ROAD TRIP

SIMON SPOTLIGHT

New York London Toronto Sydney New Delhi

SIMON SPOTLIGHT

An imprint of Simon & Schuster Children's Publishing Division

1230 Avenue of the Americas, New York, New York 10020

This Simon Spotlight edition May 2020

Text by May Nakamura

TM & © 2020 RTR Production, LLC, RFR Entertainment, Inc. and Remka, Inc., and PocketWatch, Inc.

Ryan's World and all related titles, logos and characters are trademarks of RTR Production, LLC, RFR Entertainment, Inc. and Remka, Inc.

The pocket.watch logo and all related titles, logos and characters are trademarks of PocketWatch, Inc. All Rights Reserved.

Photos and illustrations of Ryan and Ryan's World characters copyright © RTR Production, LLC, RFR Entertainment, Inc. and Remka, Inc.

Stock photos and illustrations by iStock

SIMON SPOTLIGHT and colophon are registered trademarks of Simon & Schuster, Inc.

For more information about special discounts for bulk purchases, please contact Simon & Schuster Special Sales at 1-866-506-1949 or business@simonandschuster.com.

Manufactured in the United States of America 0320 LAK

2 4 6 8 10 9 7 5 3 1

ISBN 978-1-5344-7767-4

ISBN 978-1-5344-7768-1 (eBook)

ALABAMA

Capital: Montgomery
The Yellowhammer State

Our first state is Alabama, where NASA's US Space & Rocket Center is located. Here you can see rockets that have actually flown to space!

Many important people who stood up for civil rights were born in Alabama. Rosa Parks became an important figure for African American rights after she refused to give up her bus seat to a white man. Helen Keller, a deaf and blind woman, fought for the rights of many people, including women and people with disabilities.

ALASKA

Capital: Juneau
The Last Frontier

Alaska is home to Denali, the tallest mountain in North America. Alaska is also where the Iditarod, a sled dog race, takes place every year. The race usually takes eight or more days to finish. That's a long time!

Did you know that Alaska is sometimes called the Land of the Midnight Sun? That's because during the summer in some parts of Alaska, the sun doesn't set until after midnight!

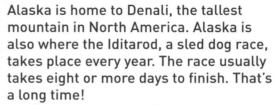

ARIZONA

Capital: Phoenix
The Grand Canyon State

Arizona is a great place to see desert plants like the prickly pear cactus. But perhaps the most famous place in the state is the Grand Canyon, a deep valley made from many layers of red rock. In some places, the canyon is more than a mile deep!

Here's another fun fact about Arizona that you might not have known. It officially became a state on Valentine's Day of 1912!

ARKANSAS

Capital: Little Rock
The Natural State

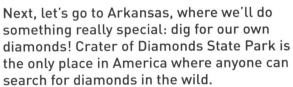

Next, let's go to Arkansas, where we'll do something really special: dig for our own diamonds! Crater of Diamonds State Park is the only place in America where anyone can search for diamonds in the wild.

By the way, do you know why Arkansas and Kansas are spelled similarly but pronounced differently? Both state names come from the Kaw American Indian tribe, which is sometimes called Kansa. Arkansas uses the French pronunciation of the tribe ("AR-can-saw"), while Kansas uses the English pronunciation ("CAN-zus").

CALIFORNIA

Capital: Sacramento
The Golden State

California has the largest population of any state, and it's one of the largest in size, too. Many tech companies are located in Northern California, including Google and YouTube. I love posting videos online!

In Central California, farmers grow a lot of food, like almonds, garlic, and grapes. In Southern California, you'll find great beaches for surfing . . . and famous people in Hollywood, if you're lucky!

COLORADO

Capital: Denver
The Centennial State

Phew! I can feel our car working hard as it climbs up the mountains. Denver, the state capital, is 5,280 feet—or one mile—above sea level. That's why it's sometimes called the Mile High City. People like hiking and camping in Rocky Mountain National Park, which is also near Denver.

Colorado is nicknamed the Centennial State because it became a state in 1876—exactly one hundred years, or a century, after the United States became its own country.

CONNECTICUT

Capital: Hartford
The Constitution State

Connecticut's shoreline isn't just good for beaches. It's great for fishing, too! You can also see a lot of beautiful lighthouses along the coast.

If we drive away from the ocean, we'll be able to visit Lake Compounce in Bristol. It's not just an ordinary lake . . . it's a lake *and* the oldest amusement park in the United States! What are some of your favorite things to do at an amusement park?

DELAWARE

Capital: Dover
The First State

Delaware is called the First State because it was the first one to agree to the US Constitution and officially join the country. Delaware is also sometimes called the Blue Hen State after its state bird. The Blue Hen actually has blue feathers!

Today Delaware is popular for its pretty beaches along the Atlantic Ocean. What do you like to do at the beach?

FLORIDA

Capital: Tallahassee
The Sunshine State

When you hear of Florida, you might think of its great amusement parks and beaches. But did you know that Florida is the only place in the world where you can see crocodiles and alligators living together in the wild? You can see both of them in Florida's Everglades National Park.

Let's stop and get something to drink. How about some orange juice? Florida produces the oranges for more than 90 percent of America's orange juice. Yum!

GEORGIA

Capital: Atlanta
The Peach State

Right above Florida is the state of Georgia. I can't wait to eat all the good food that it's famous for: juicy peaches, sweet pecans, and yummy peanuts!

Here's a fun fact: Georgia has a swamp called Okefenokee, and it's one of the largest swamps in America. I hope there are no swamp monsters in there, though!

HAWAII
Capital: Honolulu
The Aloha State

Aloha! Hawaii is the only state that has two official languages: English and Hawaiian. It's also the only state made entirely of islands, which were created from the lava of underwater volcanoes. How awesome is that?

Hawaii has warm temperatures that are perfect for swimming, surfing, and other water sports. I love swimming—what about you?

IDAHO
Capital: Boise
The Gem State

Idaho produces a lot of potatoes . . . more than any other state in the country! Here, you can also find more than seventy kinds of gemstones and more than four hundred kinds of birds.

What time is it in Idaho? It depends on what part of the state you're in! The northern part of Idaho is in the Pacific Time Zone. The southern part is one hour ahead in the Mountain Time Zone.

ILLINOIS

Capital: Springfield
The Prairie State

Some people call Illinois the Land of Lincoln because President Abraham Lincoln lived here for more than thirty years. You could also call it the land of pumpkins, since it produces more than any other state!

In 1871 the Great Chicago Fire burned through the city and destroyed thousands of buildings. But many people helped Chicago rebuild, making it into the big city that it is today.

INDIANA

Capital: Indianapolis
The Hoosier State

Vroom, vroom! We're now entering Indiana. A popular race called the Indy 500 takes place here. I like racing—I even have my own racing video game!

Let's drive to the northern part of Indiana to visit America's newest national park, the Indiana Dunes. These sandy beaches along Lake Michigan stretch for miles and miles!

IOWA

Capital: Des Moines
The Hawkeye State

Iowa sits between two big rivers: the Missouri River to the west and the Mississippi River to the east. The rivers provide water for farms. Iowa farmers produce the most corn in the United States!

I'm feeling hungry, so let's stop for some peanut butter and jelly sandwiches. Did you know that the man who invented sliced bread was from Iowa? That's cool!

KANSAS

Capital: Topeka
The Sunflower State

Amelia Earhart, the first female pilot to fly across the Atlantic Ocean by herself, was born in Kansas in 1897. Pizza Hut was also "born" in Kansas—its first store opened in Wichita in 1958. I looove pizza!

By the way, did you know that there are two cities in the United States called Kansas City? One of them is in Kansas, and the other is in Missouri . . . and they're right next to each other. How confusing!

KENTUCKY

Capital: Frankfort
The Bluegrass State

Kentucky is home to Mammoth Cave, the largest cave system in the whole world! It has underground lakes, rivers, and awesome rock formations.

What's cooler than that? There's actually a small part of Kentucky that's not connected to the rest of the state. People who live there have to drive through Tennessee to get to other parts of Kentucky. That's wild!

LOUISIANA

Capital: Baton Rouge
The Pelican State

Now it's time to visit Louisiana, where jazz music was created. Louis Armstrong, a famous jazz musician, was also born and raised in this state.

Louisiana is known for its Cajun and Creole food, which has been influenced by the many immigrant communities who have lived here. But perhaps Louisiana is most famous for its celebration of the Mardi Gras holiday, complete with parades, costumes, and masks!

MAINE

Capital: Augusta
The Pine Tree State

Next we're going to Maine, in the northeast corner of the United States. It has more than three thousand islands near its coast, where you can catch a lot of seafood. In fact, Maine produces more than 80 percent of America's lobsters.

Maine is also one of the coldest states in America . . . which might be why earmuffs were invented here! Brr!

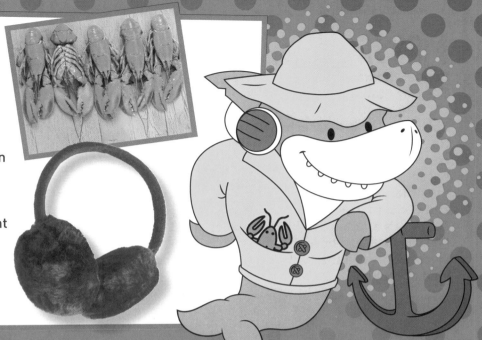

MARYLAND

Capital: Annapolis
The Old Line State

I hope you're ready for more seafood, because Maryland is famous for its blue crabs. Their claws are actually blue! Many of the blue crabs live in the Chesapeake Bay, which is the country's largest estuary. That's a fancy word for where a river meets the ocean.

During the War of 1812, a man named Francis Scott Key watched a battle happening in the Chesapeake Bay. It inspired him to write "The Star-Spangled Banner"!

MASSACHUSETTS

Capital: Boston
The Bay State

The next stop is Massachusetts. The famous Boston Tea Party, where the American colonists protested British taxes by throwing tea into the harbor, took place in 1773. And the first battles of the American Revolution happened at Lexington and Concord in 1775.

Here's another fun historical fact about Massachusetts: chocolate chip cookies were invented here in the 1930s! What's your favorite kind of cookie?

MICHIGAN

Capital: Lansing
The Great Lakes State

When you look at Michigan on a map, it's divided into two sections. The Upper Peninsula, or UP, is connected to Wisconsin. The Lower Peninsula kind of looks like a mitten! Together, they touch four of the five Great Lakes: Lake Erie, Lake Huron, Lake Superior, and, of course, Lake Michigan.

Since we're on a road trip, it only makes sense to drive through Detroit. Henry Ford, a businessman who helped popularize cars in America, started his company here in 1903.

MINNESOTA

Capital: Saint Paul
The North Star State

Minnesota is known as the Land of 10,000 Lakes . . . but they actually have 11,842! Hockey is so popular here that some people think Minnesota should also be known as the State of Hockey.

Minneapolis and Saint Paul are the two biggest cities in the state. They also happen to be right next to each other, so together, they're called the Twin Cities. Do you know any twins? My little sisters, Emma and Kate, are twins!

MISSISSIPPI

Capital: Jackson
The Magnolia State

Mississippi was named after—you guessed it—the Mississippi River! The river runs along the state's western border. Many famous people were born in Mississippi, like Oprah Winfrey, a popular talk show host and producer, and Jim Henson, the creator of the Muppets.

The magnolia is Mississippi's state flower and its state tree. Mississippi even has an entire town named Magnolia!

MISSOURI

Capital: Jefferson City
The Show-Me State

It's hard to miss the Gateway Arch in St. Louis. It's 630 feet tall, and it is a monument for the United States' western expansion in the 1800s.

That includes the Pony Express, a group of horseback riders who delivered mail from Missouri to California in the 1860s. They would travel more than 1,800 miles in ten days! Today you can visit the beginning of the Pony Express National Historic Trail in St. Joseph.

MONTANA

Capital: Helena
The Treasure State

Montana has many national parks, including Glacier National Park and part of Yellowstone National Park. About three hundred grizzly bears and six hundred black bears live in Glacier National Park.

Montana also has a Dinosaur Trail, which is a group of dinosaur museums, parks, and sites throughout the state. In some places, you can even dig for dinosaur bones yourself. Maybe you'll find the next T. rex fossil!

NEBRASKA

Capital: Lincoln
The Cornhusker State

Did you know that more than 90 percent of Nebraska's land is used for farms and ranches? They produce corn, soybeans, cattle, and more.

Nebraskans don't forget to give back to their land. They held the world's first Arbor Day in 1872, where people planted about one million trees in one day. That's a lot of trees!

NEVADA

Capital: Carson City
The Silver State

Whoa! Was that a UFO soaring through the sky? A lot of people say they've seen strange things along Route 375 in Nevada. In fact, there were so many sightings along the route that the state decided to name it the Extraterrestrial Highway.

What's spookier than that? Nevada officially became a state on Halloween in 1864! And that's pronounced "Neh-VAD-uh," not "Neh-VAH-duh"!

NEW HAMPSHIRE

Capital: Concord
The Granite State

New Hampshire is famous for its beautiful nature, especially White Mountain National Forest in the northern part of the state. It has mountains for skiing and about 1,200 miles of hiking trails to explore.

Speaking of exploring . . . Alan Shepard, the first American to travel to space, was born in New Hampshire in 1923. That's really cool!

NEW JERSEY

Capital: Trenton
The Garden State

Are you feeling hungry? Then let's stop for some food in New Jersey, the diner capital of the world! This state has more than five hundred diners, and many of them are open twenty-four hours a day.

The famous Thomas Edison made most of his inventions in New Jersey during the late 1800s and early 1900s. He invented many things, including an electric light bulb that was cheaper and lasted longer than the ones before it. You can still visit his research lab in New Jersey today!

NEW MEXICO

Capital: Santa Fe
The Land of Enchantment

Do you want to go for a ride in the air? Every year, New Mexico has the largest hot air balloon festival in the world, with more than five hundred balloons. While you're up high, you can see the landscapes that the famous artist Georgia O'Keeffe loved to paint. The state is so pretty that it's nicknamed the Land of Enchantment!

   Did you know? New Mexico's state gemstone is turquoise because the state has many turquoise mines!

NEW YORK

Capital: Albany
The Empire State

New York is home to New York City! It's the city with the largest population in the United States, and you can see the famous Statue of Liberty here.

   But there's so much more to New York State besides the city. The Finger Lakes in central New York are long and thin like fingers . . . except that there are eleven of them! And right on the border of New York and Canada is the famous Niagara Falls. It's one of the largest waterfalls in the world!

NORTH CAROLINA

Capital: Raleigh
The Tar Heel State

North Carolina is home to the Great Smoky Mountains National Park, which it shares with Tennessee. Every year the park has the most visitors of all the national parks in the country.

   The US presidents James K. Polk and Andrew Johnson were both born in North Carolina. In 1903 the Wright brothers made history in Kitty Hawk, when they successfully made their first flight in an airplane. Three . . . two . . . one . . . ready for takeoff!

NORTH DAKOTA

Capital: Bismarck
The Peace Garden State

Our next stop is North Dakota . . . and Canada, if you want! The International Peace Garden sits on the border between North Dakota and Canada, so you can take a nice walk in both the United States and Canada. The garden is the reason why North Dakota is called the Peace Garden State.

   North Dakota produces the most honey of all the states. In 2018 it made more than 38 million pounds of honey. That's sweet!

OHIO

Capital: Columbus
The Buckeye State

Are you ready to rock? Cleveland is home to the Rock & Roll Hall of Fame. You can see cool instruments, costumes, and other items used by popular rock stars.

Many famous people were born in Ohio, like Neil Armstrong, the first human to walk on the moon. There have also been seven US presidents born in Ohio: Ulysses S. Grant, Rutherford B. Hayes, James A. Garfield, Benjamin Harrison, William McKinley, William H. Taft, and Warren G. Harding.

FIRST MAN ON THE MOON

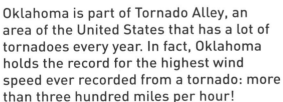

OKLAHOMA

Capital: Oklahoma City
The Sooner State

Oklahoma is part of Tornado Alley, an area of the United States that has a lot of tornadoes every year. In fact, Oklahoma holds the record for the highest wind speed ever recorded from a tornado: more than three hundred miles per hour!

People in Oklahoma have made many important inventions, like the shopping cart and parking meter.

OREGON

Capital: Salem
The Beaver State

Our next state is Oregon! It has Crater Lake, the deepest lake in the country. It can be up to 1,943 feet deep! The lake has two islands, called Phantom Ship and Wizard Island. How mysterious!

Let's get out of the car to stretch our legs and enjoy the view. If we're lucky, we might be able to spot a beaver. It's the state animal and the reason behind the state nickname.

PENNSYLVANIA

Capital: Harrisburg
The Keystone State

Are you feeling hungry? Let's stop by for some chocolate in Hershey! That's right—the town is named after the man who started one of the most popular chocolate companies in the world.

If we drive west from Hershey, we can visit Punxsutawney Phil. Legend has it that Phil, a groundhog, can predict when spring is coming. If we drive east, we can see the Liberty Bell in Philadelphia. The bell has a big crack and doesn't ring anymore, but it's still a famous symbol of America.

RHODE ISLAND

Capital: Providence
The Ocean State

Rhode Island is the smallest state in the United States. It's so small that it can fit into Alaska more than four hundred times! More people live in Rhode Island than Alaska, though.

There are a lot of fun ways to play in Rhode Island. The Flying Horse Carousel in Watch Hill is one of the oldest carousels in the country. The International Tennis Hall of Fame is in Newport. And all along the coast, Rhode Island's waters are popular for sailing!

SOUTH CAROLINA

Capital: Columbia
The Palmetto State

Do you see those trees with leaves that look like fans? They are palmetto trees, South Carolina's state tree! That's also why the state's nickname is the Palmetto State.

A lot of people like playing golf in South Carolina because the weather is nice all year. There are more than three hundred golf courses in the state! Have you ever played golf or mini golf before?

SOUTH DAKOTA

Capital: Pierre
The Mount Rushmore State

The most famous spot in South Dakota is Mount Rushmore. It's a large hill with the faces of Presidents George Washington, Thomas Jefferson, Theodore Roosevelt, and Abraham Lincoln. Each face is about sixty feet tall!

South Dakota also has Badlands National Park, where there are a lot of cool red rock formations. One of the reasons the Lakota American Indians call the area "bad" is because of its extreme weather. It can get as hot as 116 degrees and as cold as negative 40 degrees Fahrenheit!

TENNESSEE

Capital: Nashville
The Volunteer State

Music is an important part of Tennessee. You can visit the Country Music Hall of Fame as well as the Graceland Mansion, where rock star Elvis Presley lived. Singers like Aretha Franklin and Dolly Parton were also born in Tennessee.

Do you want to know another fun fact about Tennessee? It shares borders with eight other states: Kentucky, Missouri, Virginia, North Carolina, Mississippi, Alabama, Georgia, and Arkansas. It's tied with nearby Missouri for bordering the most states!

TEXAS

Capital: Austin
The Lone Star State

All this traveling is making me hungry. Should we eat some yummy Texas BBQ? Or how about some Tex-Mex food, which is a mix of Texan and Mexican cooking? What a hard decision!

Did you know that Texas used to be a country? It was its own country for nine years before joining the United States in 1845.

UTAH

Capital: Salt Lake City
The Beehive State

Utah's capital, Salt Lake City, is named after the Great Salt Lake that's nearby. It's the largest saltwater lake in the entire Western Hemisphere!

Utah is a very popular place for skiing, snowboarding, and other winter sports. Salt Lake City hosted the Winter Olympics in 2002, where the USA team won thirty-four medals. What's your favorite winter sport?

VERMONT

Capital: Montpelier
The Green Mountain State

Vermont is famous for its state tree, the sugar maple. They make about two million gallons of maple syrup every year. Imagine how many pancakes and waffles you could eat with all that syrup!

Speaking of sweet things, the Ben & Jerry's ice cream company opened its first store in Burlington in 1978. Today you can tour their factory in Waterbury and watch them make all their cool flavors.

VIRGINIA

Capital: Richmond
Old Dominion

England's first permanent settlement in North America was in Jamestown. You can still visit it today and see what life might have been like four hundred years ago.

Eight US presidents were born in Virginia: George Washington, Thomas Jefferson, James Madison, James Monroe, William Henry Harrison, John Tyler, Zachary Taylor, and Woodrow Wilson. That's more than any other state!

WASHINGTON

Capital: Olympia
The Evergreen State

Washington is known for its apples. It produces about two and a half million tons every year! It's also the biggest producer of sweet cherries, pears, and red raspberries in the United States.

If you visit Seattle, Washington's largest city, one of the first things you'll see is the Space Needle. It's 605 feet tall, and you can take an elevator up to 520 feet in the air. I hope you're not afraid of heights!

WEST VIRGINIA

Capital: Charleston
The Mountain State

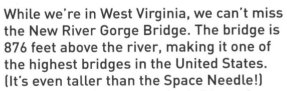

While we're in West Virginia, we can't miss the New River Gorge Bridge. The bridge is 876 feet above the river, making it one of the highest bridges in the United States. (It's even taller than the Space Needle!)

We can drive across the bridge, of course, but how would you like to go under it in a white-water raft? White-water rafting is when you ride in a small raft on a fast-moving river. West Virginia has a lot of great rivers where you can do it!

WISCONSIN

Capital: Madison
The Badger State

Minnesota might be called the Land of 10,000 Lakes, but Wisconsin actually has more than fifteen thousand! And lakes aren't the only thing that Wisconsin has a lot of. It makes the most cheese in the country—more than three billion pounds a year! I wonder how many pizzas you could make with that much cheese!

Wisconsin's nickname is the Badger State because it is the state animal. You can also see the badger on the state flag!

WYOMING

Capital: Cheyenne
The Equality State

Now we've made it to Wyoming, where most of Yellowstone National Park is located. Yellowstone was the first national park in the United States. It's famous for the Old Faithful geyser, which shoots hot water and steam from the ground on a regular schedule. That's why it's called "faithful"!

A lot of animals live in Wyoming, like bison and bears. We might actually see more animals than people here, because Wyoming is the state with the lowest population!

WASHINGTON, DC

Before our trip ends, we can't forget to stop in Washington, DC. It's the capital of the United States! The capital is where many important government activities take place. The US Congress makes laws, the Supreme Court justices decide on important court cases, and the president lives and works in the capital.

Washington, DC, has many monuments, memorials, and museums. It also has the Library of Congress, which is the largest library in the world!

We've finally reached the end of our road trip. Wasn't that a lot of fun? I feel like I learned so much about the United States! Which state do you live in? What would you like to tell me about your state?

Thanks for joining me on my road trip across America. I hope I see you again soon!

RYAN'S ALL-AMERICAN QUIZ

Now that you've gone on a road trip with Ryan,
can you answer these questions about the United States?
Don't forget to check your answers on the last page!

1. What kind of music was created in Louisiana?
   A. classical
   B. pop
   C. jazz
   D. rock

2. Where did the 2002 Winter Olympics take place?
   A. Utah
   B. Arkansas
   C. Nebraska
   D. Oregon

3. Which place has the largest library in the world?
   A. North Dakota
   B. Tennessee
   C. Kansas
   D. Washington, DC

4. Why is Delaware called the First State?
   A. It was the first state to join the United States.
   B. George Washington was born in Delaware.
   C. It had the first amusement park in the country.
   D. It was the first state that we visited on our road trip.

5. How were the Hawaiian Islands formed?
   A. They broke off from California.
   B. They were made from volcanoes.
   C. They floated up from the ocean floor.
   D. Nobody knows.

6. Which state has the largest population?
   A. Washington
   B. Illinois
   C. Pennsylvania
   D. California

7. Who was the famous inventor who worked in New Jersey?
   A. Marie Curie
   B. George Washington Carver
   C. Thomas Edison
   D. Betsy Ross

8. Where is the Rock & Roll Hall of Fame?
   A. Ohio
   B. Virginia
   C. Oklahoma
   D. Vermont

9. What fruit is Georgia famous for?
   A. lemons
   B. oranges
   C. peaches
   D. strawberries

10. Florida is the only place where you can see which two animals living together in the wild?
    A. alligators and antelopes
    B. crocodiles and alligators
    C. beavers and badgers
    D. penguins and grizzly bears

ROAD TRIP ACTIVITIES

When you're on a road trip, try these activities to make the car ride more fun!

ALPHABET GAME

Try to spot each letter of the alphabet in order. You can find the letters on signs, buildings, and anything else outside your car window. Play this game by yourself or race against someone else to be the first person to spot the whole alphabet.

LICENSE PLATE GAME

Look at the license plates of the other cars on the road. Keep count of how many different state license plates you see.

20 QUESTIONS

Choose one person to play "it," and have them think of an object. Everyone else in the car takes turns asking up to twenty "yes" or "no" questions about the object. If they can't guess the answer after twenty questions, the person playing "it" wins!

MAP ACTIVITY

Carefully pull out the poster at the end of this book. Then use markers, crayons, or colored pencils to complete the activities below!

- What state do you live in? Mark it by drawing a red star on it.
- Have you ever lived in any other states? If so, mark them with a green star.
- What states have you visited before? Mark them with a blue star.
- What states would you like to visit someday? Mark them with a purple star.

Answers: 1.C 2.A 3.D 4.A 5.B 6.D 7.C 8.A 9.C 10.B